Create your own learning plan

Example: My learning plan for writing better reports.

I need to go through the following areas to make sure that I am getting them right:

1. Identifying different types of reports (Section 1)

2. Preparing and planning a report (Section 3)

I need to increase my confidence and spend the most time on this area:

3. Drafting and editing a report (Section 4)

Write your own learning plan here. The questionnaire on page 4 will help you get started.

_____

_____

_____

_____

_____

_____

_____

_____

_____

_____

_____

_____

_____

_____

_____

_____

_____

_____

Section 1

IDENTIFYING TYPES OF REPORTS AND BASIC REPORT STRUCTURE

The purpose of reports

We write to communicate an idea or a piece of information to another person or other people. A report is a piece of writing which has a specific purpose. Generally speaking, there are four main reasons or purposes for writing a report. These are:

- to record information
  For example, a report which provides a record of an accident at work.
- to influence decision making
  For example, a report which sets out the problems with an old computer system and proposes that money should be invested in a new system.
- to initiate action
  For example, a report proposing that car park charges should be increased.
- to persuade people to do something.
  For example, a report on traffic conditions which demonstrates the advantages of cycling to work instead of going by car.

Reports vary in length, style and layout. For example, you might quickly handwrite a short report about what you saw at an accident that has just happened. Alternatively, you might write a lengthy formal report after carrying out an investigation which lasted several weeks.

Reading reports

We all read reports of different types, whether it is a report in a newspaper or magazine or a report about an accident at work, for example. Thinking about what helps you to understand other people's reports, and what doesn't help you, will guide you in your own writing.

Activity 1

Think of different reports you have read recently (e.g. a committee report, a colleague's report, an accident report).

What do you find difficult or unhelpful when you read other people's reports?

WRITING BETTER REPORTS. LEARNING FOR WORK Series. © Workbase Training

What helps you to understand other people's reports?

You will find the feedback to this activity on page 19.

_____

_____

Structure for a basic report

Reports are a way of communicating information using a particular format or structure. The format varies, depending on the type of report and its purpose. For most purposes, the following structure provides the best way of presenting the information in a report.

1. Introduction
This should explain briefly to your readers what you are going to write about (the topic) and why you are writing the report (the purpose).

2. Main points
This is where you present your findings/information and any conclusions you draw from them. Your information should be set out in a logical order, such as sequence of time or order of importance.

3. Conclusion
This is a brief summary of your main points. Nothing new should appear at this stage.

4. Recommendations
These should lead directly from your conclusion. If there is more than one recommendation, they should be listed separately, so that they can be considered individually rather than being accepted or rejected as a whole.

5. Appendices
This is where you put any other information, e.g. graphs, facts or tables, which relates to or enlarges on the subjects covered by the report, but is not needed to understand the main focus of the report. Each appendix is given a number or letter and is referred to by this title (e.g. you would say 'see Appendix A').

Note: Sometimes it may be helpful to start the report with a summary.

Activity 2

You work for a local council and have to write a report for your supervisor, Hayley Walters, about your team's policy on building new bus shelters. The report will be circulated to councillors and will also be available to interested members of the public.

You have the following information:

Bus shelters are not built on request.
Headteachers have to make a request, giving details of pupil numbers, for school bus shelters.
Visits have to be made to non-school sites for surveys to take place.
Shelters are built on a priority basis only.
No area has priority over other areas.
Priority is based on bus-stop usage.
Distance from other bus shelters is taken into account.
People are asked to contact the Technical Officer, Zarim Singh, on 0800 45689 if they have any queries or feel that their bus stop is used sufficiently to come within the policy.

On a separate sheet of paper, draft an outline for a report, using the format below, based on this information.

Introduction
Main points
Conclusion
Recommendations

You will find the feedback to this activity on page 19.

To know what to put in each section refer to 'Structure for a basic report' above.

Key Learning Points

Reports are written for various reasons, of which the main ones are:
to record information
to influence decision making
to initiate action
to persuade people to do something.

Reports may vary in length, style and layout.

A report is easier for the reader to understand if it follows a simple structure based on a clear beginning (introduction), a middle (containing relevant facts in order) and an end (a summary of what you have said).

Even a short report should follow this structure. This makes it easier for you to organise your information and clearer for the readers to understand.

WRITING BETTER REPORTS. LEARNING FOR WORK Series. © Workbase Training

Section 2 — GENERATING IDEAS FOR A REPORT

Sometimes you will find that gathering ideas for a report is the first hurdle you come to. When you are not sure what points to include and how to group them, there are two useful ways of generating ideas. These are known as 'brainstorming' and 'mind-mapping'.

Brainstorming

Brainstorming is an excellent method of generating a lot of ideas. It is particularly effective when two or more people are involved.

Stages

- Write the main aim or subject of your report at the top of your paper.
- As ideas come to mind, write them down. Write quickly and keep going.
- Do not discuss the ideas until the flow stops.
- Group the ideas and select headings. Consider which of these ideas are important to the main purpose of your report and what order you should put them in.

Mind-mapping

Mind-mapping is similar to brainstorming, but has the added advantage of showing the links between ideas.

Stages

- Write the main aim or subject of your report in a circle in the centre of a piece of paper.
- Draw a line extending away from the circle and write down your first idea as close as possible to the line.
- Add other ideas about the same subject along the same line or on lines branching from it.
- Continue adding to the subject until you have covered everything you can think of.
- Go back to the central topic and think of another aspect or theme which is linked to it.
- Develop ideas along other branches in the same way.
- Check each idea to decide whether it should be along a new line or an offshoot of a previous one.
- Look at your main topic and branches and consider which ideas are important to the main purpose of your report and what order you should put them in.

An example of mind-mapping

Planning the office move.

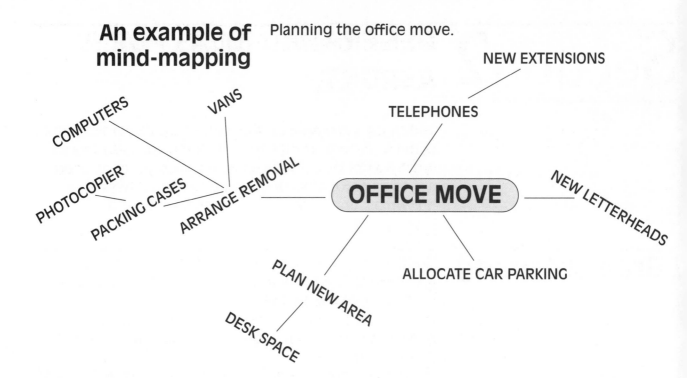

Activity 3

You have been asked to come up with an outline plan of a report. Draw a mind-map or jot down brainstormed ideas to show how you would draft your plan. Choose your subject from the following:

- 'The need for continuous training within my company.'
- 'The need for everyone to continue developing themselves.'
- If you already write reports as part of your job, take a subject you know you will have to write a report on in the near future.
- Ask your supervisor or a colleague for a topic.

Try to do this activity with a friend or colleague as you will generate more ideas this way.

Take a separate sheet of paper for this activity.

Key Learning Points

If you are not clear about the content or headings of your intended report, then mind-mapping and brainstorming are ideal ways of gathering ideas. These processes will help you to think about the topic from all angles.

These activities will also help you to group your ideas under headings and find a logical order for your material.

Section 3 PREPARING AND PLANNING A REPORT

Five steps in writing a report

The following steps are very important in any writing you do. If you follow these steps they will help you to write clearly and concisely and achieve your purpose.

- Prepare.
- Plan.
- Draft.
- Edit.
- Proof-read.

In this section we will look at the first two steps – preparation and planning.

Preparing your report

Before you begin to write your report or gather together your material, try to find the answers to the following questions.

What is the purpose of the report?
   What is the reason for writing the report?
   What is it hoped that the report will achieve?

What is the intended readership?
   Who will read the report?
   What do the readers want to know?
   How much do the readers already know about the subject?

What is the scope of the report?
   What themes and topics need to be included?
   What material should I leave out?
   Should I include recommendations?

How soon does the report need to be written?
   What is the deadline for its completion?

All these questions are very important. If you do not know the answers you may not communicate the right information or place the right emphasis on it. For example, if you know the purpose of the report you will have a clear idea about what to include, because you will select material that helps you achieve this purpose. If you know the scope of the report – e.g. machinery breakdowns in 1998 – you will limit your material to that particular period of time.

Planning your report

Once you have answers to the questions considered above, you will be able to move on to planning and organising your material. Very few people would be able to write a report without thinking about their topic and organising their material first. Planning is therefore another very important stage in report writing.

Planning ensures that:

- you give the readers the information they need to know
- your material is set out in a logical order
- your writing is correct, to the point and complete.

Giving readers the information they need

The questions in the preparation stage will help you decide what information you need to include.

Step 1: Define the purpose of writing

What is the purpose or reason for writing? You may find it helpful to go back to the beginning of the booklet where we identified five reasons for writing a report. If you are not clear about the purpose of writing or what you hope to achieve, then your report is likely to be confusing and difficult to understand.

Step 2: Identify your readers

Think about the people who will read your written work. Do they have specialist knowledge of the subject? If your readers are a mixture of specialists and non-specialists then you will need to make sure that your writing meets the needs of both groups.

Step 3: Consider what the reader wants to know

This will depend on the purpose and scope of the report. For example, if you are writing about the demand for leisure facilities in your local community in order to get funding for a new sports hall, your readers will want facts and statistics which demonstrate that your community is a priority area for funding.

Setting out material in a logical order

If you write down information simply in the order it comes into your mind this may not be the most logical sequence. First make a note of all the points you want to include then decide on the sequence in which you are going to present the information. If you have a mental block or need some ideas to start yourself off, you might want to try brainstorming or mind-mapping (see page 9).

You should ask yourself what information your readers

need to know first, second, third, etc. If you are writing about an incident which has occurred, the most logical order is the sequence in which events happened. Similarly, a working process would be described in the order in which it is carried out.

In most cases the most important point that helps your report to achieve its purpose will be your first point. You will then move on to your next most important point and so on.

Ensuring that your writing is correct, to the point and complete

It is important that you check all your facts and figures, so that the information in your report is accurate.

Present all the facts as clearly as you can, and make sure the information is complete. Use simple language and short words to aid understanding. Use longer words only where they are needed to describe something more accurately.

If you are explaining something which is complex, try to use short sentences (say, between seven and twelve words long) to make the information easier to understand.

Activity 4

Take the topic in Activity 2 and prepare and plan a report on it.

Refer back to Activity 2 for the main points you need to include. Then look at the questions listed under 'Preparing your report' at the beginning of this section and write down answers to as many as possible. Next consider the three points under 'Planning your report' and make brief notes.

You will find the feedback to this activity on page 20. Take a separate sheet of paper for this activity. Keep it safe as you will need to use this information again.

Key Learning Points

- [ ] Preparation and planning are vital stages in the process of writing a report because they will help you to achieve your purpose.

- [ ] Careful preparation enables you to know exactly why and for whom you are writing a report.

- [ ] Careful planning enables you to gather all the relevant information and make sure that it is presented clearly and in a logical order.

Section 4

DRAFTING AND EDITING A REPORT

Overcoming writer's block

Do you still find it hard to get started? Feel panicky? Write words and then cross them out? Have difficulty finding the right word? Look up words in the dictionary? Stop! You can't write and edit at the same time: each time you stop to look up a word or think about what you have written, you lose your momentum. Try to write the whole thing first – you'll get a sense of achievement from seeing what you have written – and then edit later. The following tips may help you:

- **Write without stopping.**
  Take your major points, one at a time, and start writing. Write down everything that you can think of about that topic. Don't try to look for more impressive words or stop to evaluate what you've written. The theory is that any act of writing – pen on paper or fingers on keyboard – activates the creative part of your mind. Try it!

- **Write during your best time.**
  Write when you feel high in energy and at your freshest. Don't put it off until you feel too tired to think clearly.

- **Create an atmosphere that will encourage you to write.**
  You may need to work at home, or at least shut your office door. Unplug the phone or go to a library. It may help to set a timer for a specific period – say, 30 minutes.

Activity 5

Now it is time to draft your report. Take the topic you covered in Activity 2 and make use of the work you did in Activity 4. You may want to add some extra information to give a fuller explanation. However, don't change the facts and remember to include all the points provided in Activity 2.

You will find the feedback to this activity on page 21.

You will need to draft your report (either word-processed or handwritten) on a separate sheet of paper and attach it to the booklet. Later in this section you will find out how to edit and proof-read your report.

 WRITING BETTER REPORTS. LEARNING FOR WORK Series. © Workbase Training

Editing and proof-reading your report

Once you have drafted your report you can then go back and edit it. Editing involves looking at your writing critically and changing words and style where necessary to make it easier to read. You may need to change the order of your points and put in headings to help the reader follow your text. You should also look at any particularly long words you have used: would a short word do just as well?

Using headings to help you

The use of headings can be helpful in both reading and writing a report.

Headings help the writer to:
• plan the material
• sequence ideas
• improve the layout
• focus the writing.

Headings help the reader to:
• gain an overview
• find information easily
• recognise action points
• read more quickly.

Use the checklist below to help you decide when to use headings.

Headings should:
• accurately describe the content of a section of the report
• flow in a logical sequence
• be positive in tone
• attract the reader's attention
• direct the reader to key points.

Activity 6

Look at the 'End of Course' report below. Edit the report to simplify the language and include appropriate headings. We have highlighted a number of things you could think about changing; you may wish to change others as well. There are no strict rules: the aim is simply to make it easier to read.

End of Course Report: Communication Skills Course

Herewith the report requested by the communication skills tutor to indicate **how worthwhile** a pilot course has been, the type of things that were included and conclusions and recommendations for changing the structure and content of the next course.

The course **commenced** in September and **concluded** in December.

Communications in many forms were studied and tried out on the course. Good rules of listening, who to communicate with and effective verbal and non-verbal communication. Personal development was covered by the following sessions – How to become more assertive and putting your points of view across.

The course **endeavoured** to present a basic introduction to maths. This **comprised of** extracting information from graphs, percentages, fractions and long division.

The written work was quite **comprehensive** and **was made up as follows**: the planning and structure of written communications, letter writing, instructions, memos, form filling and report writing. **Allied to this** was how to use a dictionary and reference books to their **greatest** potential.

This course has been **a real eye opener**, the **complexity** of the subject has been enlightening. The talking and discussion were very good. I found the course of great help and would advise other people to consider **contributing to the programme**. I would recommend that the course be longer and open to all members of staff who wish to **participate**.

You will find the feedback to this activity on page 22.

Proof-reading your work

You should proof-read all your writing, looking for common mistakes such as:

- spelling/typing errors (check with a dictionary or a spellchecker)
- missing words
- wrong punctuation
- lack of sense.

You need to concentrate on one area at a time: you cannot proof-read for all these things at once. Read a document first for sense, then go back and concentrate on spelling, typing errors, missing words and punctuation.

Activity 7

Go back to the report you drafted in Activity 5 and edit it. Use the checklist below to focus your editing. When you have done this, proof-read your report.

Editing checklist
Check that you have:

- kept it brief and to the point
- included all the facts
- used short words rather than long ones
- kept sentences short
- divided your writing into paragraphs
- used terms that are easily understood
- used headings
- made the report look presentable.

You should also remember what we said about the structure of a report in Section 2. Make sure your report has:

- **a clear beginning** (the reason for the report and any background information)
- **a middle** (your main points or findings)
- **an end** (your conclusions and recommendations).

Key Learning Points

☐ Drafting is the process of writing down your ideas.

☐ After preparing and planning your report, you will have gathered your material and put it in a logical order. This provides the basis for drafting your report.

☐ Don't worry about checking spelling or changing words at this stage. Just keep writing.

☐ Editing and proof-reading are the final stages in report writing.

☐ Edit your writing to check that it is clear and easy to follow.

☐ Keep words and phrases simple and sentences short. Use headings where appropriate.

☐ When proof-reading, check for correct spelling and punctuation, words missing or duplicated, correct grammar and sense.

ActionPlan

Identify the areas that you need to work on to improve your report writing by filling in the questionnaire below.

Stage	Yes	No
Preparation When you write a report do you find out: • why you are writing it? • who will read it? • when it is needed?		
Planning Do you start by: • gathering all relevant information? • putting the material into logical order?		
Drafting Do you concentrate on getting your ideas written down quickly without reviewing as you write?		
Editing Do you review your draft, correcting spelling, etc. and cutting unnecessary information?		
Proof-reading Do you read over your work to check that it makes sense and contains no mistakes?		

If you can answer yes to all the questions you should be writing effectively. Include any areas that you are uncertain about in your plan of action.

Mini Project

Look at some reports that you have received recently or any you come across at work in the next few weeks.

Look closely at:
• the structure (Is there a beginning, middle and summary?)
• the language (Do the words make it easy to read?)
• the sequence (Is the information presented in a logical order?)

Make photocopies of three or four of these reports and use different coloured pens to highlight the good and bad points.

WRITING BETTER REPORTS. LEARNING FOR WORK Series. © Workbase Training

FeedBack toActivities

FEEDBACK TO ACTIVITY 1
You may find the following things difficult or unhelpful when reading other people's reports:
Text rambles or doesn't get to the point, points difficult to follow, no headings, too brief, purpose of report not clear, not properly set out, too long, language difficult to understand.

You may find the following helps you to understand other people's reports:
Points clear and easy to follow, clear purpose, short and concise, language easy to understand, useful headings, tidy layout.

FEEDBACK TO ACTIVITY 2
Introduction
The purpose of the report, i.e. to provide information on your council's policy for building bus shelters.

Main points
Main policy
Bus shelters are not built on request.
Bus shelters are built according to priority.

Criteria for determining priorities
Priority is based on bus-stop usage.
No area has priority over other areas.
Distance from other bus shelters is taken into account.

School bus shelters
Headteachers have to make a request, giving details of pupil numbers, for school bus shelters.

How we find out if a bus stop should have priority
Visits have to be made to non-school sites for surveys to take place.

What to do if it is felt that a bus stop is sufficiently used to be given priority

Conclusions
Summary: the priority basis of the policy; the criteria for deciding if a bus stop is a priority.

Recommendations
None. The report is to provide information.

Don't worry if your report outline is not in this order. There is always more than one correct way to write a report. People also have different writing styles.

FeedBack toActivities

FEEDBACK TO ACTIVITY 4
Preparing your report
What is the reason for writing the report?
To provide information on the council's policy relating to bus shelter provision.

What is it hoped that the report will achieve?
It will answer people's questions and they will know there is a fair process.

Who will read the report?
Members of the public, councillors and the team supervisor.

What do the readers want to know?
They want to know exactly what the policy is and what they should do if they think their bus stop should have priority.

How much do the readers already know about the subject?
Some people may know what the policy is, others will know nothing about it.

What is the scope of the report?
The scope of the report is simply to outline what the policy is and let people know what they should do if they have a query or want to find out whether their bus stop is considered a priority.

What material should I leave out?
Any technical information relating to highways legislation. This is not necessary for the purpose of the report.

Should I include recommendations?
This is not required.

What is the deadline for its completion?
What date has your manager given you? When will the report be available to readers?

Planning your report
Giving readers the information they need
The reader wants to know: what the policy is; whether there are any special cases; what they should do if they think that their bus stop comes within the policy.

What is the purpose of writing the report?
To provide information on the council's policy relating to bus shelter provision, in order to answer people's questions and make them aware that there is a fair process.

WRITING BETTER REPORTS. LEARNING FOR WORK Series. © Workbase Training

Identify your readers
Councillors, members of the public, team supervisor.

Setting out material in a logical order
The most important point first
Bus shelters are not built on request.
The policy is that bus shelters are built according to priority.

Explaining the policy – the next most important point
Priority is based on bus-stop usage.
No area has priority over other areas.
Distance from other bus shelters is taken into account.

How the council decides if the bus stop should have priority
Visits have to be made to non-school sites for surveys to take place.

Exceptions to the policy
Headteachers have to make a request, giving details of pupil numbers, for school bus shelters.

What to do if it is felt that a bus stop is sufficiently used to be a priority

Ensuring that your writing is correct, to the point and complete
Look at your language, punctuation, length of sentences and grammar. Is your writing easy to understand and follow?

FEEDBACK TO ACTIVITY 5
Here is an example of a report. Remember that if yours is different it does not mean that it is wrong. Everyone has their own style of writing. Check that you have included all the main points.

Report to: Hayley Walters, councillors and members of the public

From: Zarim Singh

Date: 1 February 1999

Subject: Policy Statement on the Provision of New Bus Shelters

Introduction
The purpose of this report is to provide information on the council's policy on the provision of new bus shelters.

FeedBack toActivities

It is intended that this information will be made available to councillors and to members of the public.

The main policy on the provision of bus shelters
It has always been the council's policy that bus shelters are not built on request. Bus shelters are provided at priority sites only. Priority sites are those which have the most usage, both at peak times and throughout the day. No area is considered to be a priority over any other, except in terms of bus stop usage.

Visits are made to sites for surveys to take place to find out whether a particular site should have priority. The surveys record usage at different periods throughout the day.

In determining the level of priority, we also take into account the proximity to other bus stop shelters.

Exceptions to the policy
Headteachers have to make a request for school bus shelters, giving details of pupil numbers. There is no site visit, unless non-school passengers are involved or there is a dispute about usage.

What to do if it is felt that a bus stop is sufficiently used to be a priority.
Requests for new bus shelters should be made to Zarim Singh, Technical Officer, on 0800 45689. If possible, the request should be accompanied by some indication of bus stop usage. Further information on the policy can also be provided by Zarim Singh on the above number.

Conclusion
The council's policy on bus shelter provision is based on priority need. Priority need is assessed according to usage throughout the day. Site visits are made to carry out surveys of usage. To find out more about the policy or to request a bus shelter, please contact the council's Technical Officer on the above number.

FEEDBACK TO ACTIVITY 6
This is just one possible version of the report. It doesn't matter if yours differs from this: everyone has a different style. Try to get someone to look at your work and comment on what you have done.

**End of Course Report: Communication Skills Course
Introduction**
A report has been requested by the communication